D1710833

WITHDRAWN

Mail Carrier

HUNTINGTON CITY-TOWNSHIP
PUBLIC LIBRARY
200 W. Market Street
Huntington IN 46750

by **Dana Meachen Rau**

Reading Consultant: Nanci R. Vargus, Ed.D.

Marshall Cavendish
Benchmark
New York

Picture Words

 boxes

 mail

 mail bin

mailbox

 mail carrier

 mail truck

A  brings .

A  gets from a .

A  puts in

the .

A empties the .

10

A  sorts the .

A  drives a .

ᴴᴺᴛᴵᴹᴳᵀᴼᴺ CITY-TOWNSHIP
ᴸᴵᴼ LIBRARY
Ƭ. ʜ̲arrel Stree·
·ʜʳᵗᵒʳ, ᴵᴺ 46750

14

A  brings letters.

16

A brings .

A  is busy.

drives
> moves something from place
> to place

empties (EMP-tees)
> takes out

sorts
> puts in order

Find Out More

Books

Macken, JoAnn Early. *Mail Carrier.* Milwaukee, WI:
  Weekly Reader Early Learning Library, 2003.
Trumbauer, Lisa. *What Does a Mail Carrier Do?* Berkeley
  Heights, NJ: Enslow Elementary, 2005.

Videos

Burton, LeVar. *Hail to Mail.* GPN, 2003.
Warner Vision Entertainment. *There Goes the Mail.*
  Kid Vision.

Web Sites

American Philatelic Society: Just for Kids
  www.stamps.org/kids/kid_StampFun.htm
National Postal Museum
  www.Postalmuseum.si.edu/

About the Author

Dana Meachen Rau is an author, editor, and illustrator. A graduate of Trinity College in Hartford, Connecticut, she has written more than two hundred books for children, including nonfiction, biographies, early readers, and historical fiction. She loves checking the mailbox outside her home in Burlington, Connecticut.

About the Reading Consultant

Nanci R. Vargus, Ed.D., wants all children to enjoy reading. She used to teach first grade. Now she works at the University of Indianapolis. Nanci helps young people become teachers. She likes her friendly mail carrier, but her dog Cosmos barks as soon as he gets near the house.

Marshall Cavendish Benchmark
99 White Plains Road
Tarrytown, NY 10591-9001
www.marshallcavendish.us

Copyright © 2008 by Marshall Cavendish Corporation
All rights reserved.
No part of this book may be reproduced in any form without written consent of the publisher.

All Internet addresses were correct at the time of printing.

Library of Congress Cataloging-in-Publication Data

Rau, Dana Meachen, 1971–
Mail carrier / by Dana Meachen Rau.
     p. cm. — (Benchmark rebus)
Summary: "Easy to read text with rebuses explores the job duties of mail carriers"—Provided by publisher.
Includes bibliographical references.
ISBN-13: 978-0-7614-2620-2
1. Letter carriers—Juvenile literature. I. Title.
HE6241.R38 2007
383'.145—dc22
2006101724

Editor: Christine Florie
Publisher: Michelle Bisson
Art Director: Anahid Hamparian
Series Designer: Virginia Pope

Photo research by Connie Gardner

Rebus images, with the exception of mail bin and mail carrier, provided courtesy of *Dorling Kindersley*.

Cover photo by Joe Sohm/Alamy

The photographs in this book are used with the permission and through the courtesy of:
Journal-Courier/Steve Warmowski, p. 2 (mail bin); Joe Sohm/Alamy p. 3 (mail carrier); *Corbis*: Henry Diltz p. 5;
The Image Works: Sonda Dawes p. 7; Geri Engberg pp. 9, 15; Lee Snider p.19; *PhotoEdit*: Mary Kate Denny pp. 11, 13;
JupiterImages: Index Stock Imagery, Jeff Dunn p.17; *Getty Images*: Stone/Lawrence Migdale p. 21.

Printed in Malaysia
1 3 5 6 4 2